WOMEN
WHO
TRUST

SIMPLE AND PRACTICAL TIPS TO
CREATE A POWERFUL LEGACY,
GROWTH, AND IMPACT.

Featuring

**BOLD FEMALE LEADERS FROM
AROUND THE WORLD**

ISBN: 979-8-9897865-5-8 (Paperback)
ISBN: 979-8-9897865-6-5 (Hardcover)
ISBN: 979-8-9897865-4-1 (EPUB)

BARRIERS

I know you're looking at me
But do you really see me?
Are you threatened?
Am I suspicious?
Because I look different

I know you're probably judging me
But these Whispers are misleading

I feel a shaking in my bones
See your Eyes cold as stone
If I run… will it ever change?

Barriers …. Barriers
Pushing through barriers
I gotta change the way I see you
If you're ever gonna see me

Barriers …. Barriers
Pushing through barriers
We gotta love a little harder
We gotta hold each other stronger

I know you don't hear your words
Or the way that they hurt
As they're playing
Over and over and over again in my mind…

As my children find me
Laying on the floor
Tears streaming down my face
Trying to open up my heart to you

Barriers …. Barriers
Pushing through barriers
I gotta change the way I see you
If you're ever gonna see me

Barriers …. Barriers
Pushing through barriers
We gotta love a little harder
We gotta hold each other stronger

Can we find the footsteps in the dark
To where there's nothing but love

Barriers …. Barriers
Pushing through barriers
I got to change the way I see you
If you're ever gonna see me

Barriers …. Barriers
Pushing through barriers
We gotta love a little harder
We gotta hold each other stronger

Pushing through barriers
Pushing through barriers

Breaking down barriers
Breaking down barriers

Music written by Izdihar Jamil and Drew Lawrence
Music composed by Drew Lawrence
Singer is Izdihar Jamil

To hear the song, go to:
https://www.izdiharjamil.com/songs

Table of Contents

Introduction

The Checklist

I posted a job request at a reputable platform that can help me connect with potential editors to edit and proofread one of my previous book projects. I received over thirty applicants but was able to quickly narrow it down to two people: Sebastian and Hannah.

Sebastian has a small publishing team, while Hannah mostly works alone. Upon reviewing their applications, Sebastian checked all of the boxes on my list. I wanted to work with someone who has a team so that the work wasn't dependent on just one person; there are other team members who can support him and, in turn, avoid any bottlenecks.

Sebastian also has what I need under one roof: editing, proofreading, and formatting. This would save me time to work with multiple team members to complete the book project. In his application, Sebastian conveyed professionalism and credibility in getting the job done within the timeline. To me, this was a no-brainer choice.

Then along comes Hannah, someone that I wasn't expecting. In her application, I can sense that Hannah is someone who is nurturing and actually enjoys reading stories and working on making those stories better. When Hannah submitted a sample of her previous work, it wasn't what I was expecting; in other words, it didn't fit into my checklist.

My logical side said "Sebastian" because he fulfilled my checklist, while my heart said, "Hannah." There was just something about Hannah, even though she didn't make sense and was way off from the criteria of my checklist. Still, I couldn't pinpoint what made me gravitate towards her.

Making this decision wasn't easy because I would be spending a certain period of time with them; plus, I wanted to make sure that we were a good fit. In the end, I surrendered to my logical side, hired Sebastian, and said "no" to Hannah. That made sense at the time because he fit the checklist. I told myself that everything was going to go smoothly with this project.

I wish!

The Opposite

It turns out that Sebastian and I were not a good fit. Several mistakes were made, and I feel like the editing process needed more thought and care. Instead it felt like he was just whizzing through things. I could feel my frustration building up, and I couldn't wait to wrap up the project and move on. In the end,

Sebastian and his team completed the project to the best of their ability, and we were able to publish the book. But all this while, I kept thinking, "Why didn't I listen to my heart?"

For my next project, I immediately contacted Hannah and asked her if she could help with editing and proofreading my book. I told her my requirements and shared my vision. She said YES to the project. Actually, we both said YES to each other.

When Hannah delivered her project, I was surprised by the quality, attention to detail, and care that she put into preparing the book's content to be in its best shape. She thoughtfully considered the storyline, the big picture, how things fit together, grammar, structure, and gave ideas to improve the overall content delivery of the book.

There was a point when Hannah restructured the content of the book to help things flow better, and we just love the way she did it! Since then, Hannah has been a consistent team member in helping me create quality books for myself, my friends, and my clients. Her ideas and perspective on things are valuable in creating a page-turner book that people enjoy reading.

Hannah turns out to be a great fit for me and my team. Saying 'no' to her in the first place was such a blessing because it taught me to listen to my heart even when making decisions that are illogical. Sometimes, following the checklist isn't the answer to making the best decisions.

I learned that you have to expand and go beyond the checklist to make the best decision. At times, the best decisions are counterintuitive or feel like the opposite of logic, but that's when you'll find something valuable.

Consider that you don't know everything about someone. All you have to do is be open because that person might just surprise you. Don't get boxed in with the checklist. Instead expand and see what's possible.

This is precisely the intention of this book. "Women Who Trust" is meant to guide you to see things beyond the checklist. Sometimes, we're so adamant about the structure, checklist, or protocols that we forget that there is a whole lot of untapped potential and resources outside of that.

The bold and brilliant authors in this book have demonstrated their stories, ideas, and tips to help you expand your personal, professional, and business life. It's not easy to let go and trust the signs, but when you do, you'll see that it always leads you to something better and, at times, the best decisions that you can make.

Here's a little teaser on what you can expect from reading this book.

Dr. Izdihar Jamil, Ph.D. - Follow the Signs: Dr. Jamil, a former Computer Scientist turned Visibility Expert and TEDx Curator, shares insights on making bold business decisions aligned with your heart's calling. Learn how to recognize signs and muster the courage to follow through.

Selina Lopez Hinojosa - Overcoming Inferiority Complex: As a Transformation Coach and TEDx speaker, Hinojosa delves into overcoming addiction, embracing your fear and shame, and finding one's place in the world, inspiring readers to embrace their unique journey.

Anjani Amriit - From Shadows to Light - The Path from Self-Doubt to Self-Trust: Amriit, a Thought Leader, explores breaking free from societal expectations to embrace one's true self, fostering a deeper sense of self-trust and purpose.

Brenna Davis - Rebuild Your Self-Trust to Rebuild Your Career: CEO and Environmental Scientist Davis reflects on the importance of seizing opportunities, challenging the tendency to hold back, and trusting oneself to pursue dreams by giving yourself a shot.

Deb Rosman - Poetry: A Self-soothing Secret: Rosman, a Poet and Corporate Wellness Advocate, shares how grief and poetry intertwine, offering healing and solace, encouraging readers to explore diverse art forms for emotional well-being.

Heather Langer - Together We Can Make a Difference: Langer, Founder of ReeseStrong, Inc, emphasizes the significance of self-trust during challenging times, urging readers to stay resilient and committed to their passion that they truly believe in.

Ilona Kotelnikova - Power of Small Steps: Kotelnikova highlights the power of continuous movement and trust in the process, encouraging readers to take small steps toward their goals without looking back.

Janis Schiffner - Believe, Receive, Be Grateful, Repeat: Schiffner, a Market Sales Manager and Coach, shares insights on focusing on positivity, gratitude, and personal development to manifest abundance and joy in life.

Monica Ward - Do The Opposite: Energy Healer and Intuitive Ward explores fostering meaningful connections through empathy and understanding, advocating for kindness even in challenging interactions.

Pamela G. Bradley - Self-Doubt to Self-Trust: Bradley, a Certified High-Performance Coach™, and Master Hypnotist, empowers readers to embrace their creative power in shaping their destiny through self-belief and expression.

Tracy Smith - Power of Prayer + Belief: Spiritual Specialist Smith shares her journey of trusting herself through adversity, including divorce and homelessness, inspiring readers to navigate challenges and create a fulfilling life through prayer and belief.

Each chapter offers actionable insights and heartfelt wisdom, inviting readers to trust themselves, embrace authenticity, and embark on a journey of personal and professional growth. Dive into "Women Who Trust" and discover the keys to creating a powerful legacy, growth, and impact in your life.

This is not just a feel-good book but also contains practical tips and doable action steps to help you move forward in making a powerful impact and leaving a legacy. You'll feel like someone is holding your hand throughout the process and nurturing you in the best possible way because we can about your journey. It is such an honor and pleasure to be part of your world and knowing that you're reading this book tells us so much about who you are and what you are committed to.

Remember, the checklist isn't everything. Trust, expand, and tap into a world of possibilities- that's where the magic happens.

Best wishes,

Izdihar

Visibility Expert | TEDx Curator

https://www.izdiharjamil.com/

CHAPTER ONE

Follow the Signs

Dr. Izdihar Jamil, Ph.D.
Visibility Expert, Author, and TEDx Curator, USA

*"Be open to receiving the signs, and when it is being shown
to you, follow through."*
~ Dr. Izdihar Jamil

The Worry

I was sitting on an uncomfortable black sofa in a hospital room in Malaysia with my MacBook on my lap. My dad, Ayah, was recently admitted to the ICU due to health complications. I flew back from California when I received the news to look after him during his recovery. As Ayah was taking his nap, I would be working on my book "Speak With Influence" to channel my worry into something productive.

The hospital environment was very stressful. There were constant visits from the nurses, doctors, family members, friends, and guests. There were also times when Ayah had to go through multiple tests, from MRI to ultrasound. Every time Ayah had to go through some tests, I would get worried. Focusing my energy on writing my book helped me manage my stress level.

At the hospital, I constantly asked God for guidance on my next business move and which direction I should take. My logical mind directed me to help people write their solo book projects so they can use them to grow their businesses and make a big impact.

Once Ayah was given the all-clear from the doctor and was home, I started creating marketing strategies to direct people to my Masterclass on how they can write a powerful solo book to win clients and influence sales. The intention of the Masterclass was to give value, teach something beneficial, and then invite them to work with me on their solo book.

I would post on social media, do short reels about the benefits of becoming a bestselling author, and nurture my mailing list. On the day of the Masterclass, a few ladies showed up, and I was excited. I shared with them my best content on writing a powerful book to grow their business and then presented them with an offer to work with me.

A few days went by. Guess how many people signed up? ZERO.

I was thinking, "What's going on? Why aren't there any sign-ups? Am I really not good at what I do?"

Doing the Logical Thing

I ask God again for guidance. You see, all this while, God has been showing me guidance. He was directing me to create an anthology book, where I have the opportunity to collaborate with amazing people and help multiple people to share their voices in the book at the same time. But I chose not to listen because I thought that was not the right business move for me. At that moment, it was logical for me to help people with their solo book because, in my mind, I thought it was easier, and I could make more money from it. So, I focused my energy on marketing the solo book projects.

This time, I decided, "Why not?" Since there were no sign-ups for the solo book project, I have some free time. I get to experiment and be creative in testing things out. There were two book titles that I came up with, "Influential Trailblazers" and "Women Who ____". The blank was just a blank, I didn't know what word to put it in there. My previous book was "Women Who Lead," and upon research on Amazon, there were many other books on similar topics. I wanted something different but meaningful.

Then, the word "TRUST" came to me through prayers, meditation, and analysis. Hence, this book's title, "Women Who Trust" was born. As I was designing the book cover mockup, I felt that it needed a symbol. I personally don't like symbols or graphics on my book cover because I find them distracting, but I had a strong pull to put a symbol on the "Women Who Trust" book cover. Upon reflection, I decided to put a blue butterfly on the cover. I discovered that a butterfly is a symbol of growth, expansion, spirituality, and transformation, and I thought, "It fits."

The Unexpected

Armed with two book covers, "Influential Trailblazers" and "Women Who Trust," I started to test things out on social media and my mailing list. Out of the two books, "Women Who Trust" had the most engagement and feedback, which kind of shocked me! I was expecting "Influential Trailblazers" to be the people's choice. Based on feedback, there's something about the word "TRUST" and the blue butterfly that attracted people to the book.

Taking that feedback as a positive sign, I created a simple sign-up page. I wanted to create an experiment to see if people would want to collaborate with me on this project by writing one chapter using a writing formula that I have prepared.

Since I was still in Malaysia taking care of Ayah, I didn't want to do a sales call, masterclass, or training. Basically, it was all the things that I was taught to do in my business. I wanted to create a conversion process, turning potential clients into paid clients in the simplest way possible without doing any of those things. Once I figured out a method, I started out with my existing clients and people with whom I have a relationship. Within the same day, two people said YES! And then more people said YES!

The guidance that I was purposely ignoring turned out to be the BEST guidance. It was how this book was born! All the women and the stories in this book came alive because I finally chose to listen to the signs and follow them through.

As for the solo book project, you know, the one where no one signed up... Unexpectedly, I had women reaching out to me wanting to work with me on their solo book projects! More so because I have let go of the solo book project idea and was focusing on creating the best experience for "Women Who Trust." When you trust the guidance and follow through, you'll start to see that it's an opening to many other pathways, even the opportunity that you thought failed.

Key Lessons

The essence of this chapter can be boiled down to two things- the openness to receive the signs and the courage to follow through the signs, even when it seems illogical.

Power Summary

Here are the highlights of this chapter:

1. Fill in the blank. Follow the _____.
2. Ask God for guidance, and when it is shown to you, follow through.
3. When you trust the guidance and follow through, you'll start to see that it's an opening to many other pathways.

Action Steps

Follow through these three steps to help create trust and expansion in your decision-making process:

1. Take a moment and say, "Guide me and show me the signs for making the best decisions."
2. List one sign or feeling that you have received or are experiencing. For example, mine was the feeling of creating the anthology book project for "Women Who Trust."

3. List one action that you can take to get a result from that sign or feeling. For example, mine was to create two book covers and post them on social media.

Don't overthink it. Be open to receiving the signs, and when they are shown to you, follow through. Trust that it'll lead to something great, far beyond your wildest imagination.

Here's to loving, surrendering, and trusting the process,

Izdihar

About

Dr. Izdihar Jamil, Ph.D.—#1 International Bestselling Author of Are You Visible?, TV Show Host and Visibility Expert—has appeared on FORBES, Fox TV, and TED.com. She helps leaders to be SEEN, HEARD, and CHOSEN as the go-to experts in their field with proven, predictable, and effective methods. She's also the Curator for TEDxHuntingtonBeach. Izdihar is featured in the book "Heroes, Leaders and Legends" with Oprah, Jack Canfield, and Deepak Chopra. She lives in California with her husband and children. She loves baking and reading.

More info on Izdihar: www.izdiharjamil.com

Dedication: To my family and friends who support me no matter what. To Laura, who I miss dearly. To BH, who's been with me every step of the way. To the Pillow Talkers and the Eason team for encouraging me to play for big dreams and be my best.

Reviews

"Izdihar, trust me, you have the magnetic personality who turned my worry into happiness of helping others build values!" – Emily Lee, Student, Malaysia

"Izdihar touches souls with her unwavering faith, gentle spirit and steadfast belief! She illuminates the path for others, especially us the women, teaching us to embrace life's uncertainties with grace and gratitude, for in every trial lies an opportunity for growth, and in every blessing, a reason to rejoice." - Maria Hani Mustaffa, Doctorate Candidate, Malaysia.

"Izdihar's words and insights are a beautiful reminder of what's possible when we trust our inner wisdom" - Cindy Warden – Women's Potential Expert, USA

CHAPTER TWO

From Shadows to Light - The Path from Self-Doubt to Self-Trust

Anjani Amriit

Thought Leader, Expert in Conscious Leadership and Women's Workplace Empowerment, Australia

The Pain

Curled in a fetal position, a gut-wrenching stomach pain so severe that I keep passing out, I lie helpless on a hospital bed. Sweat pours down my face as panic and exhaustion set in. I'm close to collapse.

This is my third hospital visit this month. I'm an enigma to the hospital staff. They can't find anything wrong with me.

My head is triumphantly telling me how much of a 'loser' I am. That I have gone 'bat shit crazy.' That I should be ashamed of myself for wasting the doctor's time with my trifling problems.

The Fear

The last five years of my sixteen-year career as a corporate lawyer in the top law firms in the world have been arduous and, at worst, soul-crushing. You see, I never felt good enough to be there.

Raised in an immigrant working-class family in Yorkshire, England, I was the daughter of a shepherd. How could I ever match up to the elite of my white, male, privileged, tailored suits and power tie wearing peers? Truth was. I couldn't. Or so I believed.

Every day that I walked through the imposing doors of the fifty-five-story steel tower office building that was my workplace, a monument to power and prestige, I felt the sting of my own inadequacy.

In the vast expanse of the gleaming marble halls and bustling corridors, I stood out like a sore thumb—a mixed-race skinned woman amidst a sea of white male power suits. I felt I had to constantly prove myself worthy of such esteemed company, but nothing I said or did was ever good enough.

I worked longer and harder than everyone else, surpassing even the partners of the firm.

It still wasn't enough.

I wasn't accepted. I was constantly ignored, judged, gossiped about, and generally cast aside like some dirty, terrible mistake. I became so wracked with shame that I would hide in my office all day, avoiding speaking to anyone. Never trusting that I could ask for help. I never shared how I genuinely felt with anyone due to the fear of being seen as weak or incapable and being cast out like the black sheep from this white herd of intelligentsia.

So, I drove myself relentlessly, pushing dangerously beyond my limits. I was a wreck, teetering on the brink of burnout…and this is how I, once again, found myself in the accident and emergency ward.

The Revelation

The following day, as I sat in my shame-filled office, the weight of inadequacy holding me to ransom, I spent the tiniest excuse of a moment reflecting on my life.

To be clear, this was an act of sheer desperation rather than a genuine attempt at introspection. I was drowning in shame, feeling lost and confused. I had left myself with no other option.

I confronted myself with some terrifying questions...

Why was I doing this to myself?

Was this really what I dreamed of for my life growing up as a child?

Was this success really making me happy?

As I sat in this never-before moment of self-reflection, a realization dawned upon me. I had been trying so hard to fit into a mold that was never meant for me. I had ticked all the boxes. Done all the right things you were supposed to do. But never once had I questioned if those 'right things'… were right for me.

I had allowed society and the fear of others' judgment to put me in a nondescript, stifling, brown cardboard box. I had abandoned my true self, who loved drawing, painting, creative writing, and helping others, to live a life dictated by others' expectations. Worst of all, I had done this to myself!

In this lucid moment of clarity, I made the choice to break free from the now obvious paper-thin cardboard box of other people's expectations and trust in myself—trust in who I really was, deep down, when no one was watching. I realized that my value didn't come from conforming to the expectations of others but from embracing the real me behind the mask I wore for so long to please others. I had finally come home to myself.

From that day forward, I vowed to trust in my uniqueness, now understanding that it was my greatest strength. As I stepped out of the shadows of fear and self-doubt, I discovered a newfound sense of confidence, excitement, passion, and purpose.

The Insight

Life always offers us chances to learn and grow, building our self-worth and trust so we can be authentic in every aspect of our lives.

When we lack self-trust, we rely on meeting others' expectations, which is exhausting and hides our true selves. This has serious consequences, leading to insecurity, fear, and anxiety about making mistakes.

Trust allows us to let go of the need to control what other people think, say or do. Trust empowers us to embrace life with an open heart and mind. It inspires us to foster deeper, more meaningful relationships, take risks, and grow in ways we never thought possible.

Trust is the foundation of a fulfilling and authentic life.

Power Summary

Opportunities for Growth: Trusting ourselves gives us the opportunity for personal exploration and discovery, leading to a deeper sense of self-worth, respect, fulfillment, and happiness.

The Power of Trust: Trust allows us to let go of fear, self-doubt, comparison, and control. It paves the way for us to experience deeper, trustworthy, more meaningful relationships, take new risks with confidence, and grow more in love with our unique selves.

Action Steps

Self-awareness: This is key to moving from self-doubt to trust. Reflect on your thoughts, feelings, and behaviors, noticing when self-doubt arises. Challenge unconscious limiting beliefs to shift toward a more trusting, loving life.

Self-Compassion: Treat self-doubt with self-compassion. Tell yourself, 'I'm doing my best. I'm doing great. I've got this.' Remember, it's natural to have doubts, and it's okay to be different. Self-compassion gives you wings!

Step Out of the Box: Begin by taking small steps outside the cardboard box you've unintentionally confined yourself to. Trust your intuition, celebrate your authentic successes, and watch your confidence and self-trust grow.

Answering The Higher Call

By releasing fear, inadequacy, and the need to meet others' expectations, we free ourselves to embrace the freedom of trust. Letting go of our false selves allows us to discover our true strength and courage to honor our authentic selves and our purpose.

It is through trust that our souls truly awaken.

Anjani Amritt

About

Anjani Amriit - #1 International Bestselling Author, TEDx Speaker, 7-time Award-Winning Thought Leader, and Corporate Lawyer, Anjani challenges conventional norms to deliver higher wisdom to her audiences. Specializing in helping leaders eliminate self-sabotage to unlock their full potential through her 'inner radiance' method, she inspires them to heed their unique calling, guaranteeing success. Through keynotes, mentoring programs, corporate training, and profound purpose retreats, Anjani guarantees results. Widely regarded as the 'thinking woman's champion,' her blend of corporate savvy and natural intuition makes her a sought-after authority. Anjani is regularly featured in the media, lives in Sydney, Australia, and is an avid poet, songwriter, and adventurer.

More info on Anjani Amriit: www.anjaniamriit.com

Dedication: Dedicated to all souls on the path of awakening to their true nature. May trust be your guiding light in the darkness and your strength in the face of fear.

Review

"A warm and moving chapter about breaking free from society's expectations. A cry from the soul for liberation and truth." - Tracey Spicer AM, author, broadcaster and journalist.

CHAPTER THREE

Rebuild Your Self-Trust to Rebuild Your Career

Brenna Davis, M.S.
CEO & Sustainable Leadership Expert

"Lift yourself up. Trust yourself."
~ Brenna

"I got the job!" I incredulously yelled to my husband, Haakon. I was stunned because I had just landed my dream job as a sustainability director of a $1B healthcare company. "Of course you did," he said. "You always do whatever you set your mind to." He had full confidence in me. Weeks earlier, though, when I submitted the application, I didn't have that same confidence or trust in myself. To understand why, let's rewind a bit.

I Started Out Trusting Myself

I love nature. It's not a lie or even an exaggeration to call me a tree hugger. As a skinny, red-headed kid with messy hair who preferred cutoff jeans and scuffed sneakers to dresses and jewelry, I wandered the woods that bordered my family's home. I heard the real sounds of the earth there and discovered

27

her beauty. I found secret and quiet places with deep carpets of soft moss, lingering mist, and bird songs. I learned to trust nature. And I learned to trust myself.

I decided to go to college and study environmental science to protect those types of places.

How the World Eroded My Self-Trust

What happened after college was a rude awakening. As a female scientist in a predominantly male field, I was thrust into an environment full of subtle acts of exclusion. Men mistook me for a secretary. The powers that be gave male colleagues better assignments for no other reason other than that they were male. There were some bright spots, too, of course. Some inspiring women and LGBTQAI+ folks, many of whom were both older and wiser than me, entrusted me to work on some amazing sustainability projects for Fortune 100 companies. But this was the exception.

There were two low points during this time. First, after spending a year training a newly hired male coworker, I confided in him about a better job I applied for. Before I could say, "Hey wait, I trained you!" He applied for the same job and got it. I never even got an interview. The second low moment was dispiriting and unnerving. At a conference, a

28

male mentor knocked on my hotel room door relentlessly around midnight after a party. Afraid and alone in my room, it frightened, angered, and lowered me—would this never end? While it pains me to admit it now, these two moments, and many more, eroded my self-confidence. I stopped seeking advancement in the workplace. I no longer trusted myself. I screened every job opportunity through the lens that I wasn't qualified enough. My career stalled. So I went back to school, this time for a business degree.

Just Giving It a Shot

While I was in business school, I experienced a life-changing moment. I came across an article from a well-respected business journal that reported on new research that claimed women often lack the same self-confidence and self-trust as men. That part wasn't a shock to me or to any other woman for that matter. But I was shocked to read that men often just throw their hat into the ring to apply for jobs, even when they only have a small percentage of the required qualifications. In contrast, women only apply when they feel they have most of the qualifications. The article didn't address non-binary people's experiences. It's probably much worse.

Right then and there, I promised myself that if I ever came across a dream job, I would trust myself and throw my hat in the ring, even if I didn't check all the boxes. Men didn't seem to care if they were perfect, so why should I? It was high time to trust myself and give it a go, no matter what.

Rebuilding Self-Trust to a Track Record of Success

So, we're back to where we started. After I courageously applied for a dream job, that fateful phone call came in. After some negotiation, I accepted the position. I was always capable of it – I just had to trust myself and remember those days spent in the woods, learning trust and confidence. Since then, I have been a part of executive teams of several companies, ranging from $400M in revenue to $1B, and I am now the CEO of a mid-size, privately owned company.

Power Summary

There is no panacea for the challenges that women face, but here are some lessons that helped me:

1. Trust Your Gut

    Discrimination and subtle acts of exclusion are real. Don't second-guess yourself. Trust yourself.

2. Throw Your Hat in that F***ing Ring

    Promise yourself that you'll apply for that dream job.

3. Be Support & Seek Support

    Speak up and interrupt when you see someone excluded. Seek personal support through groups of like-minded women or work with a therapist.

Action Steps

1. What is your dream job? Spend some time identifying it through journaling. Set up an internet query for that dream job.

2. Make a pact with yourself that you will fearlessly apply for your dream jobs.

3. Get support. Be an ally. Do you have a support network? If not, start building it today.

Joy & Light,

Brenna

About

Brenna Davis, M.S. is an organic food advocate, sustainable business expert, environmental scientist, and CEO of a mission-driven food company. Her work has been featured on every major news network, including live morning television. She is the two-time #1 International Bestselling Author of *She's a Boss* and *Hello Success*. She was also featured in *Global Chorus: 365 Voices on the Future of the Planet* alongside Paul Hawken and Jane Goodall. She is a sought-after public speaker on national and international stages and has spoken at the Obama White House, international climate events, on a panel facilitated by Vice

President Al Gore, and on every major network including live morning television.

More Information on Brenna: https://www.brennadavis.com

Dedication: To the future generations of women. May you always throw your hat in the ring.

CHAPTER FOUR

Poetry: A Self-Soothing Secret

Deb Rosman
Author, Speaker, and Corporate Wellness Advocate

*"In this age of extremes, the ability to self-soothe is
more important than ever, so consider poetry. Whether
it's something you write, or read the works of others,
poetry is an excellent vehicle through which you
can achieve calm and self-soothing."*
~ Deb Rosman

Receiving the Dreaded Call

Many of us have received that dreaded call…which defies the odds by often coming in the middle of the night. For me, it came late one night in October 2008.

Ring…ring…ring…

"Hello…?" I answered sleepily.

It was my sister-in-law; she didn't return the greeting; she just blurted out, "Mom is gone."

Suddenly, I sat bolt upright in bed, wide awake with the pain of grief gripping my chest so tightly I could barely breathe. Eventually—with the saddest outrush of air—I feebly uttered something like, "Is she?" I'm not sure what happened next because my world went blank.

The Importance of Grieving

I was lucky to have enjoyed loving, supportive parents my entire life. My father, Frank, was the first to make his transition from the physical in 2003, followed by my mother, Joyce, in 2008.

As cliché as it might sound, my mom was one of my best friends. Her death was far from my first rodeo when it came to processing intense grief. I had lost several close family members, including (but not limited to) my father and my sister. But this pain was almost insurmountable.

Many times, I have heard that a loss like this can never be overcome. Trusted people, people whom I know personally, have told me, "You will just have to learn to live with this for the rest of your life." How can that be true? Living with this pain isn't really living.

I questioned further: *is this what my loving parents would wish for me?* I really didn't think so, but I was overcome with grief. I read somewhere that the pain of grief comes from feeling physically pinched off from a loved one, and that resonated with me.

After wrestling with these thoughts and concepts, I eventually came to rely on a few simple modalities that allowed me to self-soothe and ultimately move forward.

Art is Always the Giver

Somehow, grief and poetry have always gone hand in hand for me. I experienced the first loss of a family member at age fifteen, and during that time, it was poetry that soothed me. Often by bringing me to tears because tears are the pressure valve to the soul. Years later, Kahil Gibran's *A Tear and A Smile* is still one of my favorite pieces and continues to soothe me.

I'm a writer, so it's no surprise that I love journaling. I find it so healing because I can transfer the pain inside my heart onto a page; there, it becomes infinitely more manageable.

Art has so many forms. Multiple art forms could transport you from your pain if you allow them to, just as journaling and poetry transport me.

Grief Should Have an Expiration

Grief is a natural, normal process, and if you are lucky enough to live a long life, it's inevitable that you will experience it multiple times. The ways that we choose—*yes, I said choose*—to grieve are as numbered as the stars in the night sky.

Physics teaches us that energy cannot be created or destroyed; it can only change form. My poet's interpretation is that when a loved one transitions from the physical world back into the nonphysical world, they take their essence along with them. This consoles me, knowing my loved ones are not gone. The spirit/soul is energy and remains intact because, like other laws of physics, it, too, is constantly expanding.

Power Summary

Self-soothing is one of the best tools in our toolkit of life skills. Actually, it is one of the many ways we can improve our lives daily, on a moment-by-moment basis. The fact that grief is unavoidable makes self-soothing even more important. Use these three keys to help work through the grieving process.

1. Understand Physics: Our spirit and/or soul cannot be destroyed; it can only change form.

2. Use Poetry/Art: Any of the arts are useful, but if you haven't specifically tried reading or writing poetry, then try it. You might surprise yourself.

3. Choose Life: After a loved one's physical transition, it's important to eventually return to living a joyful life.

I posed a question at the beginning of this article: *Would my loving parents wish for me to grieve their mortal loss for the rest of my mortal life?* I concluded that their answer would be *no*! It can be very tempting to continue to mourn the physical loss of a loved one, but what if deciding to live fully again best honors their memory?

Action Steps

Here are three simple action steps to help you achieve the power of self-soothing:

1. Get out into nature. Take a walk—even five to ten minutes outside will cause your brain to reboot.
2. Keep a journal. It is beneficial to get things out of your head and onto paper or tablet.
3. Constantly be gentle and kind to yourself. This one often trips us up—we are our own worst critics; it is time to be your best advocate.

If you're grieving right now, pay attention to your needs. Consider taking some time off work, scheduling a spa day, or doing some therapy shopping. You might want to meet with a professional therapist, but whatever you do, pursue soothing. Relax in the knowledge that this pain will pass if you allow it to. Please understand that when you do move forward, you are not forgetting but, instead, honoring.

The truth is, one cannot draw water from an empty well, so self-soothe often and always secure your own oxygen mask first.

"Secure your own oxygen mask first."

- Deb Rosman

Deb Rosman

About

Deb Rosman is an author, speaker, and corporate wellness advocate. She is an international best-selling co-author of *It is Done!* Using techniques from the Law of Attraction she teaches others to foster self-soothing during the grieving process.

Her first book, *The Grieving Heart: a collection of poetry and prose about loss, hope, and living,* which serves many as a silent companion during their grief journey. Deb became an entrepreneur at age sixty, making her a case study in reinventing oneself. She understands that the only constant in life is change and believes that we can always change for the better.

For more information, visit her website: https://debro sman.com/

Dedication: This is Dedicated to the beautiful memories of my parents, Frank & Joyce; your love lives on forever.

Review

If you're grieving the loss of a loved one, Deb Rosman's deeply compelling and profoundly moving story serves as a guiding light, illuminating the gentle path toward healing. It offers companionship and comfort, encouraging the heart to find peace and the spirit to trust in its own fortitude and resilience.

- Lindi Tardif,

Rookie and *Daughter of Apartheid* Author

Tech Founder, Lawyer, and Board Member

CHAPTER FIVE

Together We Can Make a Difference

Heather Langer
Founder of ReeseStrong, Inc

"You got this!"
~ Reese Langer

A Mother's Worst Nightmare

It was the afternoon of my 13-year-old daughter's cheer banquet. I watched her skip across the stage to receive the Social Butterfly Award. She was full of excitement and giggles as she ran back to tell me, "I wasn't going to dance across the stage, but you only live once." Those words will forever be engraved in my heart.

Moments later, she was celebrating with her teammates and ate a dessert that she thought was safe. Her throat started to feel strange, and she was having difficulty breathing. We discovered she had brought the wrong bag because her usual one didn't match her beautiful dress. This meant her medication was not with us. We immediately headed home. I don't recall how fast we were going; I just knew we needed to beat time. When we got there, she started throwing up. I quickly gave her an EpiPen shot and raced her to the ER. On the way, she lost consciousness, and her older brother attempted CPR in the backseat before carrying her lifeless little body into the hospital. They tried everything to get her heart beating as I bawled my eyes out. Lack of oxygen to her brain left her in a coma for four days before she passed away. My world crumbled. I not only lost my daughter but also my best friend.

We will always remember Reese for her sweet spirit, pure heart, and infectious smile. She lived life with the utmost kindness and innate ability to make those around her feel loved and included. She often encouraged others through their struggles with "You got this." She left a hole in our hearts that can never be filled.

What Now?

How could I move forward when it didn't seem possible? I didn't know what I would become. It would've been easy to crawl into a dark hole, fill my heart with hatred, and dwell on dark thoughts of "what ifs." I opted not to know who had catered the event to protect myself from having that much resentment towards someone. The new, unlabeled dessert was Baklava, a honey pastry with finely chopped walnuts.

We prayed for a miracle, but in reality, we were blessed to have this beautiful soul in our lives for 13 years. I was lucky to be her mother. I had to trust that some things were not meant to be understood and that this was part of a bigger plan. I wasn't sure if my smile would return. How could I be her voice? To share her story, I would have to relive that heartbreaking moment repeatedly.

#ReeseSTRONG

I had to figure out a way to make her death meaningful. It became my life mission to raise awareness and inspire change through a nonprofit called ReeseStrong, Inc. It was time to trade tragedy for triumph.

If you are passionate about advocating for causes close to your heart, keep going. Your reason is your fuel. Let that speak to you. Be the voice when others feel they've lost theirs.

The Importance of Advocacy

Can you imagine living in fear, afraid to eat because a bite of food could end your life? There are many triggers and threats that cause your mind to go into overdrive. You must be relentlessly vigilant with every snack and meal. Every 10 seconds, a food allergy reaction sends someone to the ER. It's vital for EVERYONE to understand that food allergies are serious.

A food allergy happens when your body's natural defenses overreact to a particular food molecule, and the body's hypersensitive response can lead to anaphylaxis. This is a severe allergic reaction that can occur after exposure. If not treated immediately, it can result in unconsciousness or death.

You must be your child's strongest advocate and teach them to speak up. There are many misconceptions about people living with food allergies. It is not a diet; it is a disease. It is more than just an inconvenience of not packing a peanut butter sandwich in your child's lunchbox. Parents send their children to school trusting that school policies are followed, but 25% of children have a first-time food allergy reaction there. It's crucial to collaborate closely to ensure a safe environment. Understanding helps families manage allergies confidently, recognize symptoms, and respond appropriately with an action plan.

The impact of food allergies extends beyond the immediate health risks, affecting the quality of life and emotional well-being of those affected. Food allergies are a significant and growing concern that affects over thirty-three million Americans and 1 in 13 children. Avoiding allergens can be challenging, as they can be hidden in medications and meals or mislabeled in ingredient lists. This underscores the importance of education, awareness, and preparedness. With anaphylaxis, time is of the essence, and immediate action is critical to halt the potentially fatal progression. It is important to remember: Epi First, Epi Fast.

Power Summary

1. Accidents happen, even with a well-laid plan.
2. Fill in the blanks. _____ first, _____ fast.
3. How many Americans are living with life-threatening food allergies?

Action Steps

1. Think twice about eating nuts on a plane. There is no ER at 36,000 feet.
2. Wear teal in support of Food Allergy Awareness Week in May.
3. Learn to recognize the symptoms of a food allergy reaction and how to administer epinephrine safely.

Let's work together to create a world where every child can live without fear of food allergies!

Heather Langer

✉ heather@reesestronginc.com
@ ReeseStrongInc
🌐 www.reesestronginc.com

About

Heather Langer is a resilient advocate and loving mother who tragically lost her teenager to a food allergy. Devastated by this loss, Heather is raising awareness about the dangers and advocating for greater education and resources for affected families. Through her personal experience, she has become a spokesperson, sharing Reese's story to inspire action and support. Heather tirelessly works with policymakers to push for improved labeling laws, awareness, and increased access to life-saving medication. Her courage and determination have touched the lives of many, offering solace and hope to those navigating similar challenges.

Website: www.reesestronginc.com

Visit our website for your free gift.

Dedication: To all families affected by food allergies, may your journey be filled with understanding and support. Together, let us raise awareness, promote safety, and embrace inclusivity.

A special thanks to my boys, who are my pillars of strength and my incredible man who encourages me to keep going. To my mother and the ReeseStrong board, who spend countless hours helping to raise awareness through community events. Last, but not least, thanks to my friends and family. I couldn't do this every day without your love and support.

CHAPTER SIX

Power of Small Steps

Ilona Kotelnikov MS, NBC-HWC,
Entrepreneur, Author, Speaker

"The journey of a thousand miles begins with a single step."
~ Lao Tzu

Annoying Question

Just yesterday it happened again. Somebody said, "I like your accent. Where are you from? Germany? Sweden?"

I hate answering this question. It still triggers something inside of me, and memories from my past force their way into my mind.

"I'm from Russia."

Pause.

"Aw… Really? How long have you been here? How often do you go back?"

People like making assumptions. They will easily imagine who you are and place you in a certain box. Beware if you don't fit in.

I've been living here for 12 years. I'm an American now, and I've never gone back.

So, let me be clear once and for all, and I will tell you my story.

Ground Zero

I had a good life in Russia: a husband, a lovely son, and a few pets. I had my own successful bakery and coffee shop business, great friends, and family.

Until one day, I'm divorced, and criminals are threatening to kidnap my son and take over my business.

My amazing mom took my son with her to the U.S., and I stayed to fight another day.

One year later, I left everything behind and arrived in the U.S. with just one suitcase. I'm 30 years old, and I have to start my life all over again.

I don't speak a word of English. I don't have friends, a business, or a job. My future looks dark and uncertain. Everything is new to me; I'm in complete culture shock! Food tastes sweet: potatoes, corn, and even milk. Don't even ask me about cookies and cakes, I can't eat them! They are too sweet for me.

How do you guys navigate here? How do you know whether it is south or north while driving on a freeway? Why are the traffic lights after the intersections and not before, like in my country? This discovery almost caused me to have an accident. What are ramps? Exits? I'm lost, asking for help from an 8-year-old and drawing maps in my head.

And worst of all, because I don't understand a word of English, I can't talk to people, and I don't understand them talking to me. No language, no friends, and no social connections meant loneliness and isolation. Now I know why they call foreigners -aliens. I felt like one; better to say I *was* one.

Rebuilding From Ground Zero

I'm a successful overachiever, fighter, and rebel. I felt hopeless and depressed. I was lying down on the couch, feeling sorry for myself, trying to see the way out of my misery. The past was so bright and attractive, and the future looked so dark and uncertain. Thanks to my dear son, who showed me his unconditional love and his need for me, I knew I had to keep going. Also, my Master of Science degree in Psychology gave me the tools and knowledge to create an approach, change my thoughts, and start taking action. I trusted the process, and the first action I took was signing myself up for an ESL class. That was just the beginning.

It took me 2 ½ years of taking small steps to put my life together and rescue myself from the deep, dark hole of depression without professional help. I learned the language. Around the same time, I realized that we all have the same problems as humans: with children and husbands, with parents, and at work, no matter which country we are living in or came from. I started making friends. My first and dear Japanese friend, Motoko, has been with me since we met in an ESL class back in 2012. Later, I found my first job at a psychiatry office, and I have never looked back, only forward. Since then, my future looks great and adventurous.

Never Stop Moving

I learned that even baby steps will lead you forward to wherever you want to go, just keep moving and never look back! TRUST the process.

You know that sharks are powerful creatures! They never stop moving, remaining in constant forward motion, and if they were to stop, they would die. Nature made them restless. Just as sharks must keep moving, the same is true for us. Once we stop moving, stop looking for meaning, for aims and goals, most likely we will sink into a dark, uncomfortable place that many call depression. So, don't stop. Look around, find meanings, and remember that there is someone next to you who needs you. You are just a step away from making that life-changing decision to keep moving and living.

Power Summary

Let's recap the key points from this chapter:

1. Finish the sentence. I'm unstoppable moving forward to my _____.

2. What was so attractive in the past that made me miserable in the present?

3. Instead of giving in to my depressive feelings, what did I choose to do to overcome the darkness?

Action Steps

1. Assess Your Current Situation and Define Your Ending Point: Begin by evaluating your current circumstances and clearly marking your desirable goal.

2. Establish Easily Attainable Daily Objectives: Identify simple, achievable daily goals. Complete one, then set another. These goals should be small and manageable. Continuously seek and accomplish them each day.

3. Build Relationships Through Friendship and Interaction: Cultivate friendships, connect with others, and engage in meaningful interactions.

Ilona Kotelnikov

About

Ilona K., MS in Psychology, National Board Certified Health and Wellness Coach.

Entrepreneur, empowered woman, and international mental health advocate. Author of "Give yourself a meaning" and "Living with anxiety."

My mission is to empower individuals to take the first step towards the direction they choose, and never look back!

More about Ilona:

You can find me on Facebook or www.healthysolutions consulting.com

Dedication: First, I dedicate this chapter to my family, especially to my amazing mom, Elena, and my son, Tim.

Second, I dedicate this chapter to my first friend in America, Motoko and my English teacher Mago, who helped me overcome my fear of connection and inspired me to keep learning English.

Last, I dedicate this to my dear friend and co-worker Polina M., who believed in me in my darkest moments and supported and empowered me through years of adapting to life in the U.S.

CHAPTER SEVEN

Believe, Receive, Be Grateful, Repeat

Janis Renay Schiffner
Market Sales Manager, Optimist, and Coach, USA

*"Understanding the power of positive intention and
trusting the Universe to manifest our deepest desires
by aligning our thoughts with all that is good,
has changed the course of my life."*
~ Jan Schiffner

Shock Treatment - The Trigger

None of us could have understood the impact that 2020 would have on all of our lives. Until then I was relatively happy, relatively successful, relatively healthy, and relatively wise, until I wasn't.

In 2020, I came down with what was initially believed to be laryngitis, but it didn't go away until one day on a work conference call, I couldn't speak at all.

I had gone to physicians about my symptoms before, but nothing that had been prescribed had helped. A specialist finally ordered MRIs and lab work, which is when the unthinkable happened. I was finally diagnosed as having had an early case of Covid in addition to Thyroid Cancer that had spread throughout my throat and vocal cords.

First Denial - The Doubt

One of the ways I've coped in my life is to deny reality at times. However, denying my symptoms caused the Cancer to escalate, requiring me to have five surgeries within one year. One thing I do credit to myself is that once I realize something needs to be done, I go all in. I had no desire to drag out treatment for years. I loved my life. I wanted to do all that I could to get back to my family, career, and traveling.

High Gear

I fast-tracked all the treatments that I could. It was a whirlwind of tests, physicians, specialists, and surgeries, until my tests came back showing my "new normal," and I was cancer and Covid free.

Reentry

Getting back to work and to life was not the easy reentry that I thought it would be. What had worked for me, both in life and with the people in it, had changed. While I had been home recovering, my co-workers faced their own challenges at work. There were leadership changes, and fear of the future ran rampant. I had expected to come back as a returning heroine but learned that my former sense of humor and quick comebacks were no longer deemed endearing or humorous. In fact, I received feedback that I was now found to be "lacking business acumen and came across as disingenuous." I had spent years developing my business skills as well as both internal and external relationships, yet what I returned to was not the ideal and supportive culture I had longingly dreamt of returning to.

More Change

Simultaneously, my son and his family decided to move back to California for warmer weather and career advancement. This included taking away my Granddaughter, who I had spent two days a week with for the first ten years of her life. While I was outwardly so very proud and happy for them, on the inside, I was silently heartbroken.

I had a very dark winter in 2022, and I wondered how everything now seemed upside down and out of place. I had to continue to work, and I still wanted to be in my family's lives, but how did I find light and hope in my new normal?

Darkest before Dawn

I knew that doing what I had been doing wasn't going to get me where I wanted to go. I had to pull myself out of the murky sludge of mental quicksand that I was sinking into. I was physically healthy but working on reprogramming my brain had to now become my top priority. Being depressed and feeling like an outcast were not going to give me the life I had worked so hard to return to.

DAWN - Turning Point

When the student is ready, the master will come. I was searching for something I could lean into and learn from to pull myself up and out from where I was. I found Dr. Sue Morter and Marci Shimoff, who were leading a year-long group called the "Year of Miracles." I dove into it. I listened to positive podcasts morning and evening, and they introduced me to dozens of thought leaders, including Jack Canfield, co-author with Marcie on Chicken Soup for a Woman's Soul and author of "Happy for No Reason," as well as Australian television writer and producer Rhonda Byrne who wrote the "The Secret." The Secret is based on the belief that the pseudoscientific law of attraction can change a person's life. I also hungrily gobbled up her other books, "The Power" and "The Magic." I became an insatiable reader and listener of all things about retraining your brain to become more positive and to open my mind to brighter possibilities.

DAYLIGHT

Since that time, I have learned that what we focus on (good or bad) is what we and our lives will become. This journey has taken me to find inspirational coaches of all kinds. I now start my day each day by listening to audiobooks or podcasts. I go to sleep listening to them like lullabies. I end each day with gratitude and wake up thrilled to uncover what each extraordinary new day will hold. I am excited about life and all of the new adventures ahead. I now trust and believe our minds can heal and take us to new levels of joy, prosperity, happiness, love, and gratitude for all.

Power Summary

I have learned that the more gratitude I have for what I have right now can open doors to new levels of abundance in all areas of my life. I am experiencing more success at both work and home, which now surpass pre-pandemic levels. I am now happier, healthier, wealthier, wiser, and excited about what is still ahead.

1. I believe that anything is possible when we tune into the magic and power of positivity.
2. When we give back and are grateful, our dreams chart new courses on the map of our lives.

3. When we trust that manifesting is possible, we are catapulted into a new realm of existence that exceeds even our best expectations.

Action Steps

1. Reprogram your mind. Change the channel from what your life is missing to one that expresses gratitude for all that you are and all that you have.

2. Find coaches/mentors, whether in person or via podcast, and soak up all you can to have positivity and a belief that great happiness, health, wealth, and love are possible. Do it until that trust and belief resonates in the core of your being.

3. Give back. Say thank you, be kind, be generous, and share your message freely with others to assist them on their own journey.

In Closing

Thank you, Universe, thank you, life, and thank you to our beautiful world. Thank you to those who voice their own extraordinary messages so others can also find joy, hope, laughter, and love.

My personal goal now is to share my journey and help others tap into this place of extraordinary love and light. It's all yours if you believe, achieve, receive, and are grateful for it all.

In gratitude,

Janis Renay Schiffner
"If the only thing you say in life is thank you, it is enough"
- JS

About

Janis Renay Schiffner is a three-time #1 International Best Selling Author who was inducted into the prestigious "Who's Who in America " for 2022 and 2023. Additionally, she was selected for inclusion into the "Motivation and Success Hall of Fame" and awarded "Outstanding Motivational Female Writer of the Year" by Every Woman TV in 2023. She has been a President's Club achiever multiple times during her tenure in both the Telecom and Print Industries. She is currently a Commercial Sales Manager overseeing three states. Jan shares her inspiring journey, success secrets, and key actions that she continues to draw upon to keep herself moving forward. She is now a sought-after guest for podcasts, television, and radio shows, as well as for inclusion in magazine articles for her insights on the power of positivity and optimism. Most recently, Jan was a celebrated keynote speaker for the Global Women's Power Summit and Expo, held virtually in Paris, France. When not working, you will find Jan traveling the globe, spending time in her garden, or restoring one of her 100-year-old homes with her faithful Weimaraner, Olivia Wilde, by her side.

LinkedIn: linkedin.com/in/janschiffner

Dedication: I dedicate this book to the very dear and forever lovely Linnea Kampa. Linnea, I will always see you as the extraordinary source of light and laughter that blessed all of our lives eleven years ago and every day since. Anything you want in life is yours to have! Believe it, receive it, and always be grateful for the amazing journey you are now on. Thank you, always, for being such a joyful part of mine!

Reviews

"Janis is an example of "walking the walk." Faced with numerous changes, a health crisis, and challenges in the workplace, Janis had a choice to make. She could succumb to the overwhelm or find a way to rise above. When problems get BIG, we often find solutions in SMALL decisions and SIMPLE concepts. Janis shares how she turned HUGE obstacles into opportunities with several SIMPLE yet powerful strategies. While simple doesn't always mean EASY, I have complete faith you can improve your life with the methodology she shares." - Dr. Erin Oksol, The Success Psychologist

"Jan's unwavering dedication to our community and her exceptional leadership are truly inspiring. Whenever Jan partnered with us on an event or campaign, I felt incredibly honored and excited. Jan's passion, professionalism, and commitment to making a positive impact were always evident in our collaborations. Her leadership style fostered a culture of excellence and teamwork, and I am immensely grateful for the opportunity to have worked alongside her. I will always cherish the memories of our partnership and the meaningful contributions we made together to support our mutual community. Thank you, Jan, for your outstanding leadership and for being an incredible advocate for positive change."
- Brooke Chhina, Advancement Officer United Way

CHAPTER EIGHT

Do The Opposite

Monica Ward, CMI, RMT
Energy Healer, Animal Communicator, and
Telecommunications Executive

"Life begins when you recognize YOU create it!"
~ Monica Ward

Conscious Thought + Action= Change

Exploring the transformative power of embracing opposites in our lives can lead to profound personal growth. As the famous quote goes, "The definition of insanity is doing the same thing over and over again and expecting different results." This wisdom encourages us to break free from monotonous patterns and consider the value of doing the opposite.

Once I grasped this concept and realized I had been doing the same things over and over and yet expected to see a different life, I started doing the opposite of whatever it was that I was doing. To create change, you first have to recognize things that aren't serving you. Then take action on those things to create change.

It all started with a piece of fuzz on the stairs. I was walking up the stairs, and I was going to walk past that piece of fuzz, and I realized if I did the opposite and picked it up, there would no longer be a piece of annoying fuzz on the stairs. The stairs would look better, and I would feel better.

I started doing the opposite of everything that came up. I knew my current actions weren't going to get me anywhere other than what I already had in life, so I had to do the opposite of what I'd been doing. This led to an amazing life that I created all by forcing myself to override what I *wanted* to do. I put myself into "robot mode," which stunned the normal thought process long enough to overcome the uncomfortable feeling of doing the opposite of what I naturally wanted to do.

Embracing Change Through Opposition

One of the fundamental aspects of doing the opposite involves embracing change. By intentionally veering away from our usual course, we open ourselves up to new possibilities. This approach challenges the status quo and allows for personal evolution. It's a deliberate step towards breaking the shackles of routine and monotony.

The notion of doing the opposite is closely tied to breaking the cycle of repetition. When we find ourselves stuck in unproductive habits or facing persistent challenges, the willingness to do the opposite becomes a catalyst for positive change.

When your alarm goes off in the morning and you want to hit snooze, do the opposite and jump out of bed. When you see a pile of mail on the table, don't walk past it for a week. Stop and sort it! Act on it!

It's too easy to become accustomed to seeing piles of "out of place things" and walk past them for weeks. It's difficult to stop and sort it and handle it. But you must do the opposite of what you have been doing to see change. And that rings true in every aspect of your life. If you see something that needs attention or is out of place, act on it right then and there. You will quickly find yourself surrounded by an inner peace that comes from the accomplishment of completing tasks while clearing and cleaning your space.

Relationships and Doing the Opposite

Our interactions with others play a crucial role in our overall well-being. By exploring the dynamics of relationships, you may see how doing the opposite can lead to stronger connections. Delving into communication, empathy, and understanding as key components in fostering meaningful relationships through the intentional choice of opposing actions or responses can create peace and harmony.

For instance, you find yourself speaking with someone who becomes nasty to you. You may want to react and meet them with the same opposition. But in doing the opposite, you meet them with kindness and defuse the situation. Their nastiness most likely has nothing to do with you. If you are driving and someone cuts you off on the road, meet them with kindness, understanding they surely didn't mean to do it. By being kind and taking the high road, you maintain that higher vibration to continue bringing goodness to you.

Conclusion

In conclusion, the philosophy of doing the opposite offers a unique perspective on personal growth, change, and success. By challenging ourselves to break free from the constraints of routine, fear, and ingrained habits, we open the door to a world of possibilities. As we navigate the complexities of life, let us remember that doing the opposite can be the key to unlocking our fullest potential.

Power Summary

Adopting an opposite mindset, actions, or perspectives can yield unexpected benefits, ultimately enhancing our overall well-being. It's extremely simple yet very difficult to execute at first. You must force yourself to do the opposite of what you want to do.

Action Steps

1. Stop procrastinating. Laziness is not conducive to action. You must take action to see any change.

2. If you see something that is out of place or needs attention, stop and handle it NOW.

3. Do a gut check. Is what you are doing serving you for your greatest good in that moment? Is this action going to give you the same results you've had? Is this what you've been doing over and over, while thinking you were going to change or see different results? Do the opposite.

You must TRUST yourself enough to let go of what you WANT to do and do the OPPOSITE to create CHANGE.

Love,

Monica Ward

Watch for the FULL version of this chapter, being released in Monica's upcoming book titled, "Do the Opposite."

About

Even as a child, Monica had a sense of unlimited possibilities within human consciousness. With the ability to see and manipulate energy, she could physically recognize the connectedness in all things. Monica is a Published Author, Motivational Speaker, Transformational Coach, Energy Healer, Empathetic Leader, and Animal Communicator based in Seattle.

More info on Monica:

https://www.monicawardhealer.com/

Dedication: To my beautiful daughters Alexis and Amelia. When you find yourselves outside of Peace, remember to Do the Opposite.

Review

"This is so good! Straight and to the point, just like doing the opposite. Don't think about it. Just do it, and the rewards build without you being aware of it. Fear and procrastination have been my personal roadblock from day one, and doing the opposite overrides the fear and procrastination if you commit to doing it without question." - Aaron Conant Telecommunications Senior Channel Manager, U.S.A.

CHAPTER NINE

Self-Doubt to Self-Trust

Pamela G. Bradley
Certified High Performance Coach™ and Master Hypnotist

*"Overcoming self-doubt can be easy. Find its roots
and pluck it from your garden of thoughts."*
~ Pamela G. Bradley

Weeds Sprouting in the Garden

My heart is pounding so loud I can hear it in my ears. Bu-dum, bu-dum, bu-dum. I'm shaky. I tell myself to breathe. I feel every nerve throughout my entire body pulsating. I open my mouth. I squeak out softly, "Your sweet familiar voice, like an echo from the past. All your favorite songs, but they'll soon be gone."

I did it! I sang into a real, live studio microphone for the first time! Eek! I'm not a singer.

I'm 62. I co-wrote and sang a song about my mom and our experience of an eight-year journey with Alzheimer's disease. My youngest son and I were her round-the-clock caregivers.

Some of my mom's favorite phrases from her lifetime were, "What is wrong with you?" "'Stop using your feet for thinking"; and, of course, her favorite word, "idiot." I'm guessing one of her least favorite words was "love" because when she died at 93, I never heard her say that word to anyone. When I was little, I remember her saying something to the effect that I should only use that word if I meant it.

Weeds Thriving

When I was young, my mom always told me that she had me at a "later age" so I could take care of her. Boy, did that end up being a self-fulfilling prophecy. When I was 16, she moved into my apartment. I supported her for two years, then again after my dad passed away in 2007, until her death in July 2022.

My mom's attitude and words created a battle within me. When I attempted to lose weight, succeed in law school, be in relationships, start my business, or needed to focus and fully show up for myself, I would unknowingly self-sabotage. I wouldn't show up, play full out, or do what I needed to succeed. I had a hard time making decisions because I did not trust myself. I had no idea what I wanted or where I was going with my life. I reacted to life instead of creating it.

Pulling Weeds

Starting around 2012, I dove deeply into personal development, high-performance coaching, health and wellness, and hypnosis. I ended up certified in all these areas. As I gained expertise with these tools, particularly the subconscious mind, I became aware of my self-talk, beliefs, and stories. Two main things flipped the switch from self-doubt and lack of confidence to courageously stepping out of my comfort zone and into self-trust.

First, I became aware of what I was saying to myself. I started eavesdropping into my thoughts and self-talk. Guess what I caught myself saying over and over? You got it: "What is wrong with you?" "Geez, what an idiot." Wow! What an eye-opener. Once I discovered this, I could ask myself insightful questions like, "Is there anything really wrong with you, Pam?" "Are you an idiot?" No! My mom probably picked up this from her mom or someone else. It has absolutely NOTHING to do with ME. Each time I became aware of this self-talk, I asked the questions, reframed, and released. I felt more empowered.

Second, I started songwriting and singing. Music is something I absolutely love. Not only is it a creative outlet, but it is also VERY THERAPEUTIC. What a beautiful way to capture feelings, work through problems, share a message, and, most importantly, express myself thoughtfully and beautifully. I can give the words emotion through the music and my personalized, custom instrument: my voice. Remember I told myself I wasn't a singer? Well, I AM! Every time I create something and sing it out loud, my confidence soars.

Time To Bloom = Key Lessons

I co-wrote a song with Drew Lawrence, "The Wish," for my grandkids. It carries a message for them: "You can create anything from nothing at all…a destiny that's yours to choose…don't forget who you are inside…dream bigger than the borders of the sky…never let the world eclipse your light."

These lyrics remind us that we are the creators of our destiny. No matter what anyone else tells us, believes about us, or instills in us, we can choose who we are and where we are going.

Power Summary

Let's recap the key points for this chapter:

1. True or False: Our words have the power to impact others and ourselves.

2. Fill in the blanks. Rather than be trapped in self-doubt, I found two ways to self-correct and start trusting myself. _____ and _____ .

3. We are the _____ of our own destiny.

Action Steps

Here are simple steps to create a world of TRUST.

1. Starting now, become an eavesdropper of your thoughts and self-talk. Be curious, not judgmental, about what you notice. Ask yourself if what you are thinking and saying is true or if it is a story from someone or somewhere else.

2. Find a creative outlet. Whether it is writing, dancing, painting, singing, or playing an instrument, any endeavor that allows your mind, body, and soul to create and express itself will build confidence and trust, especially if it is something you have never done before.

3. Starting today, pick one small thing daily that will stretch your comfort zone. Over time, this will strengthen your trust muscle and expose that unstoppable, courageously confident, bold woman that you always knew was inside you.

YOU create the ability to TRUST yourself.
Step out boldly with confidence and trust,

Pamela G. Bradley

About

Pamela G. Bradley is a Certified High Performance Coach™ and master hypnotist. She helps high-performers find clarity and courage to up their game and rise to their highest potential with ease and confidence. She lives in California with her dog, Max, and loves to write songs, work out, and connect with friends and family.

For More Information: www.pamelagbradley.com

Dedication: To my family and friends who have supported and cheered me on, Lisa Pezik for your inspiration, and Drew Lawrence for being my creative guide.

Review

"What a beautiful reminder of the power of our words! Pamela guides us to trust in our own unique ability, creativity, and resiliency and to pluck anything that casts a shadow of doubt while we tend to our garden of dreams." - Lisa Pezik, Off-Broadway Performer, TEDx Speaker, 2x Best-Selling Author, and Founder of Infinite Design House, www.infinitedesign house.com

CHAPTER TEN

Overcoming Inferiority Complex

Selina López Hinojosa
Transformation Coach, TEDx Speaker, and #1
International Bestselling Author

*"Trust in your own greatness, because if you
believe it, you can become it."*
~ Selina López Hinojosa

I Don't Belong Here

I'm at a fancy hotel in Westlake Village, California. I walk into a large conference room while the other Warrior Mastermind attendees also begin to trickle in. This is my first time ever doing anything remotely like this, and I'm so excited! I quickly find my seat, and to kill some time before the retreat starts, I decide to read through some of the bios in my participant folder.

The first one is a multi-platinum, award-winning artist and producer from L.A. WOW—impressive! Next is a 19x bestselling author and speaker. It's hard for me to comprehend who these people are. I continue reading page after page, and my heart sinks because I realize I don't belong here. I rush out of the conference room, then run to the nearest restroom where

I hide in a stall. I try to hold back tears as I repeat to myself, "Don't cry, Selina. Don't cry!" It takes everything inside of me, but I finally pull myself together, walk back out to the conference room, and take my seat. I regain my composure and begin to sort through my thoughts and emotions.

Inferiority Complex

I don't have a degree from a prestigious university, and I definitely haven't written any books or spoken in front of large audiences. I grew up in a small barrio in Corpus Christi, Texas. After attending just a few courses, I dropped out of our local community college due to issues with drugs and alcohol. At the time of this mastermind program, I had been sober for only a few years. All I had was a small fitness business that I had started from a shed in my backyard.

And now, in this room full of wealthy, educated people, my life seemed so inferior compared to theirs. Why would these highly successful people be interested in anything I have to say? What could I possibly contribute?

Overcomer

When the retreat starts, Bo Eason, our personal story coach, calls us up, one at a time, to share a defining moment in our lives. When it's my turn, I speak about my struggles with addiction until the day I randomly opened a Bible to a verse that instantly changed my life forever.

"Don't gaze at the wine, seeing how red it is, how it sparkles in the cup, how smoothly it goes down. For in the end, it bites like a poisonous snake. It stings like a viper." Proverbs 23:31-32

It was then that I was inspired to start my business, LIFT by Selina, which has become a well-respected Medical Exercise practice.

When I'm done sharing my story, the applause from the other participants is reassuring. I turn to Bo and wait for coaching feedback. He looks around the room and asks, "How much do y'all love this girl?" He tells me that people will follow me *because* of what I've overcome, *not* in spite of it. This powerful statement struck a chord in me. It was then that I was able to gain the confidence and courage I needed to discover my true purpose and calling.

Eventually, I did learn to trust in God's plan for me and in my own greatness. I've been blessed my whole life. Jesus saved me from a life of destruction that would've ended in death if He hadn't intervened. I have loving parents, the best husband in the world, and three awesome sons. The love and support that surrounds me is priceless!

I Deserve to be Here

Since then, I've been able to move forward with my life because I finally acknowledged the shame of my past and fear of rejection. Once I realized that the trauma I was holding onto was paralyzing me, I was able to continue the healing process and release it from my mind and body through prayers such as this, "God, please help me overcome these feelings of inferiority and trust Your plan for me to become the woman You designed me to be." I also sought mental health care and kept a regimen of proper nutrition and regular exercise.

Since then, I've become a successful CEO and entrepreneur. In 2022, I became the first Epic Fit Magazine cover model, and I've had two billboards in the middle of Times Square. In September of 2023, I became a TEDx Huntington Beach Speaker, and my first book, "Hello Success," became a #1 International Bestseller. Most recently, I've been writing and recording my own songs with a platinum-award-winning artist and producer (the same one I was so in awe of at the Mastermind).

I now know that my past does not dictate who I am today, nor does it determine my future. I'm no longer "Sick Selina," and I've learned to separate myself from her. I am Selina López Hinojosa, and I'm a new creation in Christ! Today, when I walk into an event such as the Warrior Mastermind, my heart fills with gratitude as I think to myself, "I deserve to be here."

Power Summary

Let's recap the key points from the chapter. What made me think I was inferior to the other Mastermind attendees?

1. Fill in the blanks. Bo Eason told me that people would follow me _____ of what I've overcome, *not* _____ _____ of it.

2. I had to learn to trust in God's plan for me, and what else?

Action Steps

Here are some action steps to trust in your greatness:

1. Determine who you may be feeling inferior to and acknowledge why you feel this way.

2. To release emotions such as shame or fear of rejection from your mind and body, consider prayer, mental health care, proper nutrition, and regular exercise.
3. Free yourself from the burdens of your past by giving yourself a reverse alter ego, such as "Sick Selina," and separate yourself from her.

Greatness is something that can be found in each one of us; trust that you are worthy of receiving it!

Selina López Hinojosa

About

Selina López Hinojosa was born and raised in Corpus Christi, Texas and is the founder and CEO of LIFT by Selina-Medical Exercise Center. In 2015, she overcame a 20-year addiction to drugs and alcohol. Since then, she's made it her life's purpose to inspire hope in others.

In 2022, she became the first Epic Fit Magazine cover model, and her photos were also featured on Supermodels Unlimited billboards in Times Square.

In September 2023, she became a #1 International Bestselling Author with her book "Hello Success," and did a TEDx Talk in Huntington Beach, California, titled "Living an Extraordinary Life in Sobriety."

More info on Selina López Hinojosa:

www.selinalopezhinojosa.com

Dedication: A mi familia López. Gracias por llenar mi vida de grandes recuerdos. Los amo mucho a todos.

Review

"Selina Lopez Hinojosa generously shares the hardest times of her life to help all of us realize that we, too, can overcome whatever is holding us back. This chapter is truly inspiring and sends a strong message to readers that we can accomplish anything. Unlike most successful CEOs and entrepreneurs who never show their flaws or inferiority complex, she opens up to readers to show that even a successful businessperson can still feel like they do not deserve to be in a room. Selina makes readers feel like they, too, can achieve what she has with hard work and determination. Even though she has come so far in her career, she still places herself in new situations like the Warrior Mastermind course to learn and grow her businesses. This chapter will leave readers motivated and ready to never become stagnant in our lives but to reach for our wildest dreams! Be bold like Selina!" – Hailey Gonzalez, Attorney at Law, U.S.A.

CHAPTER ELEVEN

Power of Prayer + Belief

Tracy J. Smith
Author, Energy, Emotional, and Spiritual Specialists
and Therapist

"I know I can, believe and feel I can, I will show I am."
~ Tracy Smith

The Moment of Challenge

"You have to get out of my house tonight. Your ex stopped by, and I am not putting my children in danger because of him," my friend told me as I walked in the door, sending me spinning further and deeper into shock. I was going through a divorce, and that day, everything happened at a quick pace.

My ex, who I had a restraining order against, obtained a court order to freeze my bank account. I had no money.

He confiscated the car I was using. I had no transportation.

He also accused me of embezzling from him and said I was crazy. I had a criminal charge to defend and clear.

He began stalking me. I had no safety.

And now I had no home. I was homeless.

I packed up my clothing and spent the night in a friend's car in a shopping mall parking lot. I only remember breaking down, being overwhelmed by fear, crying, asking *why me*, and constantly on alert for the safety of my life in case he found me.

The Unknown Moment

Less than two years earlier, I had sold and closed my businesses and moved to Northern California to marry my college sweetheart, even though I had no friends, family, or community support there. We eventually moved to Southern California, and the relationship became strained, then, verbally and emotionally abusive. The second occurrence of physical abuse caused me to experience an overwhelming fear of staying where I was. I realized that staying was a far greater fear than the fear I experienced at the thought of moving forward into the unknown, and I left the marriage. I had lost my own self-confidence, my faith, and my belief in a source greater than each of us: Divine Essence/God. Now, I had lost any resources I needed to defend and clear myself of his accusations successfully, let alone financially support myself.

The Moment of Inspiration

A few days later, the fear and anxiety were so overwhelming that I had to stop and breathe to pause the constant self-doubting thoughts and feelings stirring within me. It was then that I remembered what I was taught while growing up. Go to prayer first with gratitude, belief, and trust. I was thinking and feeling I was all by myself. I had forgotten my faith and belief in the Divine Essence/God, a source greater than each of us, and to pray with belief, surrender, trust, and be open to receive the answer.

My prayers were answered a few days later when a friend took me to see Rev. Dr. Tom Costa. He worked with me to put together a program and daily routine to build my faith, retrain my mind, regain my confidence, and deepen my trust in prayer. I did it daily as my Father taught: practice = permanence. I live by this routine to this day and commit to doing it daily, consistently, persistently, and gratefully. I am now a successfully self-employed licensed prayer practitioner and energy expert, teaching others the powers of the energy of prayer, gratitude, and trust to change their lives, and deepen and build their faith, confidence, courage, self-love, and perseverance.

Key Lessons

1. Start with prayer. YOU are not alone and have access to get help from a power greater than yourself.

2. Place your Trust in the power of your higher guidance and intuition. The answers to any questions you may have are within you.

3. Surrender and live with gratitude, no matter how bad the situation. Gratitude for blessings brings an abundance of blessings.

Power Summary

1. Say Yes! to starting with prayer, using prayer to connect to a source greater than you, surrender to Let Go-Let God, and trust your prayers will be answered.

2. Say Yes! to placing your trust and faith in yourself, your higher guidance, heart and intuition and getting through any current challenge or difficulty. God, our universe can do for you, what can be done through you.

3. Say Yes! to gratitude. Life happens for us, not to us. Be grateful for challenges, vulnerability, or uncertainty, as they are opportunities to grow, learn, and be a better version of ourselves.

Action Steps

1. Write down something you are presently challenged with and your doubts about your ability to successfully get through it.

2. Write a commitment/trust prayer agreement to yourself, include action steps you will take daily, and sign it. Include a daily affirmation or intention to say to yourself.

3. Practice commitment, trust, and prayers daily. Practice = Permanence.

"Trust is a fragile thing. Easy to break, easy to lose, and one of the hardest things to ever get back."

  - Peter Lerangis

About

For over 25 years now, Tracy J. Smith has worked with and on the energy of spirit, body, and mind connections to heal pain and stress, to help you find a place of relief, and to build a positive mind, strong body, and conscientious spirit. She has spent her career constantly learning and evolving into the healer and spiritual advisor she is today. Tracy is passionate about sharing her depth of knowledge and spirit with anyone who desires to grow, heal, and empower the energy within themselves.

Book: *Moments of Divine Inspiration*

Amazon: https://a.co/d/bLfiYlO

Instagram: @blissfulrelease

Facebook: https://www.facebook.com/blissfulreleasetrac
ysmith

Youtube: https://www.youtube.com/@tracysmith6426

Website: www.blissfulreleasenow.com

LinkedIn: https://www.linkedin.com/in/tracy-j-smith-ba
a9a04/

Lifewave: Lifewave.com/BlissfulRelease

Dedication: I dedicate this chapter to my loving parents. My Father for instilling in us the belief in ourselves and the confidence to do whatever we set our minds to. My Mother, who encouraged us to follow our hearts to pursue what made us happy no matter what others said. I am grateful for the loving, nurturing, and caring environment they provided my brothers and me as we grew up.

Reviews

"Tracy's words of wisdom are filled with heartfelt love that transforms our lives and inspires us all to be the best we can be every day."

- Dr. Rhonda Donahue, Author of *The Pollution Inside You.*

"Tracy's story chapter is so powerful and inspirational, allowing me to fully believe and trust in myself fully. I am not alone, it safe to surrender, Let Go- Let God, trust and accept it will all work out." - Dr. Diane Sheppard, Acupuncturist.

"Tracy's story of trusting and using the powerful tools of prayers, gratitude, and belief in herself in the journey from being homeless to successfully thriving personally and professionally is life-changing." - Micah Leslie, Attorney at Law, RCsP.

CHAPTER TWELVE

5 Action Steps to Gain Trust in Yourself

With our combined wisdom, we present a tangible takeaway from this book: a mini-coaching strategy session, curated as 'The Five Action Steps to Gain Trust in Yourself'. This practical guide will empower you to prepare for a transformative journey to trust in your greatness!

1. Perform a self-evaluation and define the starting point of your journey. Self-awareness is crucial to transition from doubts to trust. Observe your thoughts, emotions, and actions, recognizing instances of self-doubt.

2. Make a pact with yourself to prioritize your well-being by incorporating prayer, mental health support, a balanced diet, and physical activity. Reinforce this commitment through daily affirmations and intentional reminders.

3. Cultivate relationships and foster meaningful connections with others by engaging in interactive communication and fostering friendships.

4. Demonstrate self-compassion. Remind yourself of your capabilities and the normalcy of uncertainty.

Practice persistent kindness towards oneself to foster growth.

5. Starting today, make a conscious effort to step outside of your comfort zone daily, even if it's just a small step. Over time, this practice will strengthen your trust in yourself and reveal the bold, confident woman within.

Here's to an incredible journey that'll open the doors to impact, growth, and expansion!

Best wishes,

Izdihar, Selina, Anjani, Brenna, Deb, Heather, Ilona, Janis, Monica, Pamela, and Tracy

I AM NOT GONE

Even though my body gave out and I'm no longer around

I Am Not Gone

For you my child who is still so young, I pray you'll never
feel that I abandoned you or that you are all alone

I Am Not Gone

It's not just your memories of me that will keep me alive.
Although thinking about how much I love you and how
proud I am of you is good, there are other forces, factors,
helpers that will be there for you when you need me

I Am Not Gone

They will constantly come and go from your life, for there
can never be another me; but be there for you they will be
Coworkers, friends, relatives and many more providing you
with comfort, advice and care, so while it is true I've left this
realm I am still watching over you and with my helpers,
my agents if you will, I am still there to guide
you and advise you

I Am Not Gone

When you miss me, just stand silently and listen to my voice
beating inside you. My voice sings in the wind and will
resound in others too, my helpers, for

I Am Not Gone

The poem entitled I am not gone is part of a larger work that has been included in the United States Library of Congress Copy right TXu002120557 dated 2018-10-15.

Permission is granted on December 15, 2023 by Deb Rosman, author, to Dr. Izdihar Jamil for republication in the book "Women Who Trust".

www.ingramcontent.com/pod-product-compliance
Lightning Source LLC
Chambersburg PA
CBHW060331130626
46553CB00003B/977